This journal belongs to:

_____

Published by Christian Art Publishers
PO Box 1599, Vereeniging, 1930, RSA

© 2020
First edition 2020

Designed by Christian Art Publishers

Cover designed by Christian Art Publishers

Artwork © Amylee Weeks

Scripture quotations are taken from the *Holy Bible*, New Living Translation,
copyright © 1996, 2004, 2015 by Tyndale House Foundation.
Used by permission of Tyndale House Publishers, Inc., Carol Stream, Illinois 60188.
All rights reserved.

Scripture quotations taken from the *Holy Bible*, New International Version®,
NIV® Copyright © 1973, 1978, 1984, 2011 by Biblica, Inc.® Used by permission.
All rights reserved worldwide.

Scripture quotations taken from the New King James Version®.
Copyright © 1982 by Thomas Nelson. Used by permission.
All rights reserved.

Scripture quotations are from the *Holy Bible*, English Standard Version®.
ESV® Text Edition: 2016. Copyright © 2001 by Crossway,
a publishing ministry of Good News Publishers. Used by permission.
All rights reserved.

Printed in China

ISBN 978-1-4321-3278-1 (Faux Leather)
ISBN 978-1-4321-3151-7 (Softcover)

22 23 24 25 26 27 28 29 30 31 – 19 18 17 16 15 14 13 12 11 10

Be still

A Prayer Journal
for Women

Artwork by Amylee Weeks

CHRISTIAN ART
PUBLISHERS

Trust the Lord

Lord, I commit my failures
as well as my successes into Your hands.
Give me courage, strength and generosity
to let go and move on, leaving the past behind me,
and living the present to the full.
Lead me always to be positive
as I entrust the past to Your mercy,
the present to Your love,
and the future to Your providence.

St Augustine

Trust in the LORD with all your heart;
do not depend on your own understanding.

PROVERBS 3:5

Reflect on the things of the past that you might still be holding on to. Ask God to help you let them go and move on looking forward to the wonderful *future* He has in store for you.

"*Blessed*

are those who

trust in the LORD

and have made the

LORD their *hope*

and confidence."

JEREMIAH 17:7

An instrument of peace

Lord, make me an instrument of Your peace.
Where there is hatred, let me sow love;
where there is injury, pardon;
where there is doubt, faith;
where there is despair, hope;
where there is darkness, light;
where there is sadness, joy.

St Francis of Assisi

"I am leaving you with a gift – *peace* of mind and heart.

And the *peace* I give is a gift the world cannot give.

So don't be troubled or afraid."

JOHN 14:27

In what areas of your life do you need
more of God's peace? Turn to God for guidance
in becoming an *instrument* of His *peace*
in every area of your life.

You will keep in *perfect peace* those whose minds
are steadfast, because they trust in You.

ISAIAH 26:3

God is with you

If I go up to the heavens, You are there;
if I make my bed in the depths, You are there.
If I rise on the wings of the dawn,
if I settle on the far side of the sea,
even there Your hand will guide me,
Your right hand will hold me fast.

Psalm 139:8-10

"Fear not, for I am with you; be not dismayed, for I am your God. I will strengthen you, yes, I will help you, I will uphold you with My righteous right hand."

ISAIAH 41:10

Whenever you feel lonely or afraid,
remember that God is always with you.
Praise Him for being a constant companion
you can always rely on.

_____

_____

_____

_____

_____

_____

_____

_____

_____

_____

_____

_____

_____

"Be strong and courageous. Do not be afraid; for the LORD your *God* will be with you wherever you go."

JOSHUA 1:9

Create in me a pure heart

Create in me a pure heart, O God,
and renew a steadfast spirit within me.
Do not cast me from Your presence
or take Your Holy Spirit from me.
Restore to me the joy of Your salvation
and grant me a willing spirit, to sustain me.

Psalm 51:10-12

"*Blessed* are the pure in heart,
for they shall see God."

MATTHEW 5:8

A pure heart rested in God is the pathway
to *joy* and *peace.* Turn to God to purify
your thoughts, renew your spirit
and *refresh* your soul.

We know that when *Christ* appears, we shall be like Him, for we shall see Him as He is. All who have this *hope* in Him purify themselves, just as He is pure.

1 JOHN 3:2-3

Serenity Prayer

God, grant me the serenity

to *accept* the things I cannot change;

courage to change the things I can;

and *wisdom* to know the difference.

Living one day at a time;

enjoying one moment at a time;

accepting hardships as the pathway to *peace;*

taking, as He did,

this sinful world as it is, not as I would have it;

trusting that He will make all things right

if I surrender to His will;

that I may be reasonably *happy* in this life

and supremely happy with Him

forever in the next.

Reinhold Niebuhr

The LORD gives strength to His people;
the LORD *blesses* His people with *peace.*

PSALM 29:11

Prayerfully reflect on the things
in life that bother you. Release them to God,
knowing that He will take care of it all.
Now you can embrace the peace that comes with
trusting the Almighty Father.

Great peace
have those who *love*
Your law,
and nothing
can make them
stumble.

PSALM 119:165

You made me so wonderfully complex

Thank You for making me so wonderfully complex!
Your workmanship is marvelous - how well I know it.
You saw me before I was born.
Every day of my life was recorded in Your book.
Every moment was laid out
before a single day had passed.

Psalm 139:14, 16

"Before I formed you in the womb I knew you,
before you were born I set you apart."

JEREMIAH 1:5

Praise the Lord for every feature,
every talent and every aspect of you. He made you
wonderfully complex, uniquely *beautiful,*
His beloved daughter.

We are God's *masterpiece.* He has created
us anew in Christ Jesus, so we can do the
good things He planned for us long ago.

EPHESIANS 2:10

Rejoicing in God's love

Lord, I rejoice that nothing can come
between me and Your love,
even when I feel alone or in difficulty,
when in sickness or am troubled.
Even if attacked or afraid,
no abyss of mine is so deep
that Your love is not deeper still.

Corrie ten Boom

Nothing in all *creation* will ever be able to separate us from the love of God that is revealed in Christ Jesus our Lord.

ROMANS 8:39

Embrace the unfailing, never-ending *love* that
God pours over you every moment of every day.
Thank Him for His sacrifice, for offering up His Son
so that you can be eternally *loved* and forgiven.

Give thanks to the LORD, for He is good! His *faithful* love endures forever.

Psalm 107:1

All things to all people

You, O Lord, are the Help of the helpless,
the Hope of the hopeless,
the Savior of the bestormed,
the Haven of the voyager,
the Physician of the sick.
Be all things to all mankind,
every home and its needs.

St Basil

One God and *Father* of all, who is above all,
and through all, and in you all.

EPHESIANS 4:6

Think about the people around you – your loved ones,
friends, colleagues, neighbors…
How can they use God's help today? Pray to see how
you can be a comfort, or help to them.

Father of the fatherless and protector of
widows is God in His *holy* habitation.

PSALM 68:5

God knows your heart

Search me, God, and know my heart;
test me and know my anxious thoughts.
See if there is any offensive way in me,
and lead me in the way everlasting.

Psalm 139:23-24

Keep your *heart* with all vigilance,
for from it flow the springs of life.

PROVERBS 4:23

Open up your *heart* to God.
Share with Him your deepest fears, worries,
troubles and dreams. *Trust* Him to lead
you in the way everlasting.

For the
word of God
is *living* and
active, sharper
than any two-edged
sword, discerning the
thoughts and
intentions of the
heart.

HEBREWS 4:12

God is on my side

You keep track of all my sorrows.
You have collected all my tears in Your bottle.
You have recorded each one in Your book.
This I know: God is on my side!
For You have rescued me;
You have kept my feet from slipping.
So now I can walk in Your presence,
O God, in Your life-giving light.

Psalm 56:8-9, 13

The LORD your God is with you,
the Mighty Warrior who *saves*.

ZEPHANIAH 3:17

Consider the jar *God* has filled with your tears.
No tear falls in vain; no tear is overlooked. God sees your
sorrow and feels it deeply too. Praise the Lord for
His tender *love*, comfort and presence in your *life*.

Whether you turn to the right or to the left,

your ears will hear a voice behind you, saying,

"This is the way; walk in it."

ISAIAH 30:21

The light in the darkness

In me there is darkness, but with You there is light;
I am lonely, but You do not leave me;
I am feeble in heart, but with You there is help;
I am restless, but with You there is peace.
I do not understand Your ways,
but You know the way for me.

Dietrich Bonhoeffer

"I am the light of the world. Whoever follows Me will never walk in darkness, but will have the *light of life.*"

JOHN 8:12

Praise the Lord for His guiding Light,
ever-present help and understanding.

"I have come as a *light* to shine in this dark world, so that all who put their *trust* in Me will no longer remain in the dark."

JOHN 12:46

Love for others

Lord, save us from being self-centered in our prayers,
and teach us to remember to pray for others.
May we be so bound up in love
with those for whom we pray,
that we may feel their needs
as acutely as our own,
and intercede for them with sensitivity,
with understanding and with imagination.

John Calvin

Above all, *love* each other deeply,
because love covers over a multitude of sins.

1 PETER 4:8

Prayerfully consider the people in your life.
Pray that God will increase your *love* for His children,
giving you a caring *heart* for everyone,
even those who discourage you.

If we *love* each other, God lives in us,
and His love is brought to full expression in us.

1 JOHN 4:12

Praise the Lord

Great are You, O Lord, and greatly to be praised;
great is Your power, and Your wisdom infinite.
Grant me, O Lord, to know and understand which is
first, to call on You or to praise You?
And again, to know You or to call on You?
I will seek You, Lord, by calling on You.

St Augustine

Let everything that has breath *praise* the LORD.
Praise the LORD!

PSALM 150:6

Glorify the Lord with songs of praise, celebrating every aspect of His sovereignty and all He has done for you. Praise the Creator God, the Prince of Peace, the King of kings.

Sing to
the LORD
a new song;
sing to the LORD,
all the earth.
Sing to the LORD,
praise His name;
proclaim His
salvation day
after day.

PSALM 96:1-2

The Lord's Prayer

Our *Father* in heaven,

may Your name be kept *holy*.

May Your *Kingdom* come soon.

May Your will be done on earth,

as it is in *heaven*

Give us today the food we need,

and *forgive* us our sins,

as we have forgiven those who sin against us.

And don't let us yield to temptation,

but *rescue* us from the evil one.

Matthew 6:9-13

Be anxious for nothing, but in everything by *prayer* and supplication, with *thanksgiving* let your requests be made known to God.

PHILIPPIANS 4:6

Jesus taught His disciples the Lord's Prayer,
giving them the tools they need to build a more intimate
relationship with Almighty God. Prayerfully consider
Jesus' prayer and how you too can build a lasting, intimate
relationship with your *heavenly Father.*

Devote yourselves to prayer with an
alert mind and a *thankful heart.*

COLOSSIANS 4:2

Provision for your every need

Almighty God, who knows our necessities
before we ask, and our ignorance in asking:
Set free Your servants from all
anxious thoughts about tomorrow;
give us contentment with Your good gifts;
and confirm our faith that
according as we seek Your kingdom,
You will not suffer us to lack any good thing,
through Jesus Christ our Lord.

St Augustine

God shall supply all your need according to
His riches in *glory* by Christ Jesus.
PHILIPPIANS 4:19

Prayerfully ponder each of the wonderful
blessings God has poured over you.
He is the ultimate Provider,
giving His children everything they need
and never leaving them in want.

"Your *Father* knows the things you have need of before you ask Him."

MATTHEW 6:8

Seeking the Lord

O God, You are my God; earnestly I seek You;
my soul thirsts for You.
Because Your steadfast love is better than life,
my lips will praise You.

Psalm 63:1, 3

Draw near to God, and He will draw near to you.

JAMES 4:8

Earnestly seek the Lord in *prayer,*
asking Him to be the center of your life,
the *compass* guiding you every step of
the way to eternal life.

Let the *hearts* of those who seek the LORD rejoice.

1 CHRONICLES 16:10

Rest in the Lord

Grant me, O most sweet and loving Jesus,
to rest in You
above all health and beauty,
above all knowledge and subtilty,
above all riches and arts,
above all fame and praise,
above all visible and invisible things,
and above all that You are not, O my God.

Thomas à Kempis

Truly my soul finds rest in God;

my *salvation* comes from Him.

PSALM 62:1

Where do you find rest from the humdrum
of everyday life? The truest rest can only be found
in the presence of God. Spend time
in His presence, meditating on His promises
and embracing His *peaceful* rest.

"Come to Me,

all you who

are weary and

burdened,

and I will

give you rest."

Matthew 11:28

Knowing God

Eternal God, who is the light of the
minds that know You,
the joy of the hearts that love You,
and the strength of the wills that serve You;
grant us so to know You
that we may truly love You,
and so to love You that we may fully serve You.

St Augustine

Grow in the grace and knowledge of our Lord and Savior Jesus Christ. To Him be glory both now and forever!

2 PETER 3:18

To *truly love* God means to truly know
God and to serve Him with all your heart.
Meditate on His Word, getting to know God better
and better so that you might love God more deeply
and *serve Him* more earnestly.

"This is *eternal life:* that they know you, the only true God, and Jesus Christ, whom You have sent."

JOHN 17:3

All glory to God

Worthy are You, our Lord and God,
to receive glory and honor and power,
for You created all things,
and by Your will they existed and were created.

Revelation 4:11

The heavens declare the *glory* of God;
the skies proclaim the work of His hands.

PSALM 19:1

Glory to the King above all kings,
the Creator of the earth, our Father God!
Devote a prayer to *glorify* God, gratefully
pondering His magnitude, wisdom and love.

_____

_____

_____

_____

_____

_____

_____

_____

_____

_____

_____

_____

_____

_____

The Son
radiates God's
own *glory* and
expresses the very
character of God,
and He sustains
everything by the
mighty power of
His command.

HEBREWS 1:3

Drawing closer to God

O gracious and holy Father,
grant us wisdom to perceive You,
diligence to seek You,
patience to wait for You,
eyes to behold You,
a heart to meditate upon You,
and a life to proclaim You,
through the power of the
Spirit of Jesus Christ our Lord.

St Benedict

Seek the LORD your God, and you will find Him if you seek
Him with all your *heart* and with all your soul.

DEUTERONOMY 4:29

In humility, bow before God, asking Him to turn your *heart*, mind, soul and every inch of your being to Him. May you be completely focused on Him, *seeking* Him in everything you do and proclaiming His *glory* in the way that you live.

The lions may grow weak and hungry,
but those who seek the LORD lack no good thing.

PSALM 34:10

Confident in Jesus

You have been my hope, Sovereign LORD,
my confidence since my youth.
I will ever praise You.
You are my strong refuge.
My mouth is filled with Your praise,
declaring Your splendor all day long.

Psalm 71:5-8

The LORD will be your *confidence*
and will keep your foot from being caught.

PROVERBS 3:26

Confidently declare that God is Lord
of your *life*. Give Him the glory due His name,
humbly accepting His gift of *blessing,*
forgiveness and strength.

Because of

Christ and our

faith in Him,

we can now come

boldly and

confidently into

God's presence.

EPHESIANS 3:12

Putting God first

Eternal Father of my soul,
let my first thought today be of You,
let my first impulse be to worship You,
let my first speech be Your name,
let my first action be to kneel before You in prayer.
Yet let me not, when this prayer is said,
think my worship ended and spend the day
in forgetfulness of You.

John Baillie

"No one can serve two masters. Either you will hate the one and love the other, or you will be *devoted* to the one and despise the other. You cannot serve both God and money."

MATTHEW 6:24

Treasure the presence of the Lord in your *life*.
Without Him, life would be dull and meaningless.
Thank Him for being an eternal, loving presence in
every moment, every struggle, every joy.

"Where your treasure is, there your *heart* will be also."

MATTHEW 6:21

Blessings from above

Let all who take refuge in You rejoice;
let them sing joyful praises forever.
Spread Your protection over them,
that all who love Your name may be filled with joy.
For You bless the godly, O LORD;
You surround them with Your shield of love.

Psalm 5:11-12

The *blessing* of the LORD makes one rich,
and He adds no sorrow with it.

PROVERBS 10:22

Rejoice in the Lord! He has given you
an incredible joy above anything the
world could ever give you. He has given you the joy
of His love, His *forgiveness* and
eternal life with Him in heaven.

From His
abundance we have
all received one
gracious
blessing after
another.

JOHN 1:16

A lively faith

O Lord,
give us a lively faith, a firm hope,
a fervent charity, a love of You.
Take from us all lukewarmness in meditation
and all dullness in prayer.
Give us fervor and delight in thinking of You,
Your grace, and Your tender compassion toward us.
Give us, good Lord, the grace to work for
the things we pray for.

St Thomas More

I have fought the good fight,
I have finished the race, I have kept the *faith.*

2 TIMOTHY 4:7

Fervently seek the Father in prayer.
Ask Him to give you a *heart* that is on fire for Him;
a lively faith and a firm *hope* that nothing
in this world could ever break.

Now *faith* is the substance of things hoped for,
the evidence of things not seen.

HEBREWS 11:1

Always close to God

One thing I ask from the LORD,
this only do I seek:
that I may dwell in the house of the LORD
all the days of my life,
to gaze on the beauty of the LORD
and to seek Him in His temple.

Psalm 27:4

"Surely I am with you always,
to the very end of the age."

MATTHEW 28:20

The Lord has promised you this,
"Never will I leave you, never will I forsake
you" (see Heb. 13:5). He will be with you
to the very end, a constant guide to help
you, *love* you and protect you. Prayerfully
reflect on His amazing *promise* to you.

I saw the

Lord always

before me.

Because He is at my

right hand,

I will not

be shaken.

ACTS 2:25

A spirit of discernment

Renew in me the gift of discernment,
so that I can always see
the right direction in which I should go.
And give me the strength and the courage
to choose the right course.

St Basil

Let the **wise** **listen** and add to their *learning,*

and let the discerning get guidance.

PROVERBS 1:5

Ask God to give you the discernment you need to determine right from wrong, to live a *life* devoted to following and *serving* Him.

Wisdom is found on the lips of the discerning.

PROVERBS 10:13

Looking to God for help

I look to You in every need,
and never look in vain;
I feel Your strong and tender love,
and all is well again.
Enfolded deep in Your dear love,
held in Your law, I stand;
Your hand in all things I behold,
and all things in Your hand.
You lead me by unsought ways,
and turn my mourning into praise.

Samuel Longfellow

God is our refuge and strength,
always ready to help in times of trouble.

PSALM 46:1

Write down the things you are
most in need of today. One by one, give them
to the Lord, *trusting* that He will let
all things work out for your good.

_____

_____

_____

_____

_____

_____

_____

_____

_____

_____

_____

_____

_____

_____

Our *help*
is from the LORD,
who made heaven
and earth.

PSALM 124:8

God watches over you

Watch, dear Lord,
with those who wake, or watch, or weep tonight.
Tend Your sick ones, Lord Christ.
Rest Your weary ones.
Soothe Your suffering ones.
Shield Your joyous ones.
And all, for Your love's sake.
Amen.

St Augustine

The eyes of the LORD are on the *righteous,*
and His ears are attentive to their cry.

PSALM 34:15

This you can know for certain:
The Lord watches over you. He cares deeply for you
and longs to *bless your life* with His *peace.*
Open up your heart to Him in prayer, reflecting on
His tangible presence in your life.

The LORD Himself *watches* over you!
PSALM 121:5

In God's hands

If I say, "My foot slips,"
Your mercy, O LORD, will hold me up.
In the multitude of my anxieties within me,
Your comforts delight my soul.

Psalm 94:18-19

"I will never leave you nor forsake you."

HEBREWS 13:5

Bring your worries, cares and struggles to God in *prayer*. Allow Him to fill your heart with His comfort and *grace*.

"For I,
the LORD
your God,
will hold your
right hand,
saying to you,
'Fear not,
I will *help* you.'"

ISAIAH 41:13

Serving God

Teach us, good Lord,
to serve You as You deserve,
to give and not to count the cost,
to fight and not to heed the wounds,
to toil and not to seek for rest,
to labor and not to ask for any reward,
save that of knowing that we do Your will.

St Ignatius of Loyola

Serve the LORD with *gladness!*
Come into His presence with *singing!*

PSALM 100:2

Think about the ways in which you serve the Lord. Ask Him to help you know where He might want you to serve Him in the future.

Let nothing move you.
Always *give* yourselves fully to the work of the Lord.

1 CORINTHIANS 15:58

The way of the Lord

Teach me Your way, O LORD,
that I may walk in Your truth;
unite my heart to fear Your name.
I give thanks to You, O Lord my God,
with my whole heart,
and I will glorify Your name forever.
For great is Your steadfast love toward me;
You have delivered my soul from the depths of Sheol.

Psalm 86:11-13

Guide me in Your *truth* and teach me, for You are God my
Savior, and my *hope* is in You all day long.

PSALM 25:5

Write a prayer of praise to God,
thanking Him for revealing His **truth** to you.
Praise Him for His *love* and salvation.

Jesus answered,
"I am the way and
the truth and
the *life*."

JOHN 14:6